BASEBALL LEGENDS

Hank Aaron
Grover Cleveland Alexander
Ernie Banks
Johnny Bench
Yogi Berra
Roy Campanella
Roberto Clemente
Ty Cobb
Dizzy Dean
Joe DiMaggio
Bob Feller
Jimmie Foxx
Lou Gehrig
Bob Gibson
Rogers Hornsby
Walter Johnson
Sandy Koufax
Mickey Mantle
Christy Mathewson
Willie Mays
Stan Musial
Satchel Paige
Brooks Robinson
Frank Robinson
Jackie Robinson
Babe Ruth
Duke Snider
Warren Spahn
Willie Stargell
Honus Wagner
Ted Williams
Carl Yastrzemski
Cy Young

CHELSEA HOUSE PUBLISHERS

BASEBALL LEGENDS

JACKIE ROBINSON

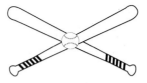

John Grabowski

Introduction by
Jim Murray

Senior Consultant
Earl Weaver

CHELSEA HOUSE PUBLISHERS
New York • Philadelphia

Produced by James Charlton Associates
New York, New York.

Designed by Hudson Studio
Ossining, New York.

Typesetting by LinoGraphics
New York, New York.

Picture research by Jennie McGregor
Cover illustration by Dan O'Leary

5 7 9 8 6 4

Library of Congress Cataloging-in-Publication Data

Grabowski, John R.
    Jackie Robinson / John Grabowski :
introduction by Jim Murray.
        p. cm.—(Baseball legends)
    Includes bibliographical references.
    Summary: A biography of the black athlete who broke the color
barrier in major league baseball when he joined the Brooklyn Dodgers
in 1947.
        ISBN 0-7910-1188-7.
        ISBN 0-7910-1222-0 (pbk.)
        1. Robinson, Jackie, 1919-1972—Juvenile literature. 2.
Baseball players—United States—Biography—Juvenile literature.
[1. Robinson, Jackie, 1919-1972. 2. Baseball players. 3. Afro
 -Americans—Biography.] I. Title. II. Series.
        GV865.R6G73 1991
        92—dc20
        [796.357'092]
[B]
90-31215

CIP

                                    AC

CONTENTS

WHAT MAKES A STAR

Jim Murray

No one has ever been able to explain to me the mysterious alchemy that makes one man a .350 hitter and another player, more or less identical in physical makeup, hard put to hit .200. You look at an Al Kaline, who played with the Detroit Tigers from 1953 to 1974. He was pale, stringy, almost poetic-looking. He always seemed to be struggling against a bad case of mononucleosis. But with a bat in his hands, he was King Kong. During his career, he hit 399 home runs, rapped out 3,007 hits, and compiled a .297 batting average.

Form isn't the reason. The first time anybody saw Roberto Clemente step into the batter's box for the Pittsburgh Pirates, the best guess was that Clemente would be back in Double A ball in a week. He had one foot in the bucket and held his bat at an awkward angle—he looked as though he couldn't hit an outside pitch. A lot of other ballplayers may have had a better-looking stance. Yet they never led the National League in hitting in four different years, the way Clemente did.

Not every ballplayer is born with the ability to hit a curveball. Nor is exceptional hand-eye coordination the key to heavy hitting. Big-league locker rooms are filled with players who have all the attributes, save one: discipline. Every baseball man can tell you a story about a pitcher who throws a ball faster than anyone has ever seen but who has no control on or *off* the field.

The Hall of Fame is full of people who transformed themselves into great ballplayers by working at the sport, by studying the game, and making sacrifices. They're overachievers—and winners. If you want to find them, just watch the World Series. Or simply read about New York Yankee great Lou Gehrig; Ted Williams, "the Splendid Splinter" of the Boston Red Sox; or the Dodgers' strikeout king Sandy Koufax.

A pitcher *should* be able to win a lot of ballgames with a 98-miles-per-hour fastball. But what about the pitcher who wins 20 games a year with a fastball so slow that you can catch it with your teeth? Bob Feller of the Cleveland Indians got into the Hall of Fame with a blazing fastball that glowed in the dark. National League star Grover Cleveland Alexander got there with a pitch that took considerably longer to reach the plate; but when it did arrive, the pitch was exactly where Alexander wanted it to be— and the last place the batter expected it to be.

There are probably more players with exceptional ability who didn't make it to the major leagues than there are who did. A number of great hitters, bored with fielding practice, had to be dropped from their team because their home-run production didn't make up for their lapses in the field. And then there are players like Brooks Robinson of the Baltimore Orioles, who made himself into a human vacuum cleaner at third base because he knew that working hard to become an expert fielder would win him a job in the big leagues.

A star is not something that flashes through the sky. That's a comet. Or a meteor. A star is something you can steer ships by. It stays in place and gives off a steady glow; it is fixed, permanent. A star works at being a star.

And that's how you tell a star in baseball. He shows up night after night and takes pride in how brightly he shines. He's Willie Mays running so hard his hat keeps falling off; Ty Cobb sliding to stretch a single into a double; Lou Gehrig, after being fooled in his first two at-bats, belting the next pitch off the light tower because he's taken the time to study the pitcher. Stars never take themselves for granted. That's why they're stars.

1

AN HISTORIC OCCASION

Thirty thousand fans crowded into the Roosevelt Stadium stands in Jersey City, New Jersey, on April 18, 1946, to watch the opening game of the International League season. The hometown Giants, a farm team of the New York Giants, were hosting the Montreal Royals, a farm team of the Brooklyn Dodgers.

But this match-up of minor league teams was something more than just another opening day. Those in attendance were looking to witness an historic event: For the first time in modern organized ball, a black man would be taking the field in a game.

Twenty-seven-year-old Jackie Robinson, the second baseman for the Royals, and the object of the fans' attention, waited in the on-deck circle as Marvin Rackley grounded out to start the game. Then Robinson approached the plate, and a sense of anticipation filled the air. He would later recall that his hand felt "too moist to grip the bat" as he entered the batter's box. Perhaps too nervous to

Robinson led the Montreal Royals to the International League pennant in 1946, winning the title by 19 1/2 games.

Robinson is greeted at home plate by Royals' teammate George Shuba after blasting a 3-run homer against the Jersey City Giants at Roosevelt Stadium.

swing, he let the first five pitches go by. The count stood at 3 and 2.

On the next pitch, Robinson hit a bouncer to the Giants' shortstop. The throw to first beat Robinson for an easy out, but he trotted off the field to a round of applause. The "great experiment"—having a black man play in the major leagues—was officially under way.

The Royals scored on a home run in the second inning, and the score stood at 2–0 as Robinson batted with two men on and no outs in the third.

Expecting a bunt, the left-handed Warren Sandell threw a high fastball. However, the Royals' manager was letting Robinson swing away. His nerves having apparently calmed down, he swung and drove the ball deep to left field. It cleared the fence 330 feet away for a three-run home run, giving the Royals a 5–0 lead. He smiled as he made his way around the bases, receiving the congratulations of his manager, Clay Hopper, when he rounded third, and that of his teammates when he reached the dugout. But Robinson's day was far from over.

In the fifth inning, he bunted his way on base,

stole second, and advanced to third on a routine ground out. With the crowd sensing they were watching an extraordinary artist at work, Robinson danced down the baseline, threatening to steal home. The newcomer's daring broke relief pitcher Phil Oates's concentration, and he balked. The umpire waved Robinson across the plate and the crowd went wild.

In the seventh inning Robinson hit a single and stole another base, as Montreal increased its lead to 10–1. In the eighth, his final at bat of the day, he bunted for a hit, moved to third on an infield hit, then scored again by distracting the pitcher, causing him to lose his concentration and commit a balk.

When all was said and done, Montreal walked off the field with a 14–1 triumph. Robinson ended the day having had a direct hand in six of the runs. Robinson made it a full day's work. He stole two bases, scored four times and batted in three runs. The *New York Times* reported, "This would have been a big day for any man, but under the special circumstances, it was a tremendous feat."

Professional baseball would never be the same.

2

FROM HUMBLE BEGINNINGS

Robinson shows the form that earned him All-America honors while a halfback at UCLA.

Jack Roosevelt Robinson was born in Cairo, Georgia, on January 31, 1919, less than a month after the death of former president Theodore Roosevelt. Jackie was the fifth, and last, child of Mallie and Jerry Robinson.

Jerry, a sharecropper hoping for a better life in Florida, deserted the family when Jackie was just six months old. Mallie, a proud and religious woman, moved the family to Pasadena, California, when Jackie was five. As the daughter of a slave, she was well aware of the difficulties faced by blacks in the Deep South and wished to make things better for her family.

The Robinsons still faced discrimination in their new home, however, because they were one of the few black families in a predominantly white neighborhood. Neighbors and local residents often harassed them. Only the strong guidance of their mother kept the children out of trouble. In many ways, life was no different in California than it had been in Georgia. As Robinson was to recall years later, "People in Pasadena were less understanding in some ways than Southerners, and they were more openly hostile."

The youngsters released their frustrations and anger by excelling in sports. Each of the five—brothers Edgar, Frank, Mack, and Jackie, and sister Willa Mae—was an above-average athlete. Mack, in fact, was good enough to compete in the 1936 Olympics, winning a silver medal by finishing second to the legendary Jesse Owens in the 200-meter dash.

Despite having such a role model for a brother, Jackie found himself headed for what could have become serious trouble. In junior high school he hung around with a gang of neighborhood trouble-makers. Fortunately, Carl Anderson, a mechanic who worked in the area, took an interest in the fatherless boy. Together with the Reverend Karl Downs, the pastor at Jackie's church, Anderson helped convince the youngster to rely on himself rather than just being one of a crowd.

Jackie's athletic talents blossomed at John Muir Technical High School. He starred there in baseball, basketball, football, and track. After graduation, he enrolled at Pasadena Junior College, where he continued to shine. On a single day—May 8, 1938—he set a junior college broad-jump record at a track meet in Claremont, California, in the morning. Immediately following that event, he led the school's baseball team to a victory in the Southern California Junior College championship game.

Naturally, his abilities attracted a good deal of attention. The University of California at Los Angeles offered him an athletic scholarship, which he accepted.

He proceeded to rewrite the UCLA record books over the next two years, becoming the first four-

letter man in the school's history. In basketball, he twice led his conference in scoring; in track, he won the national long-jump championship; in football, he was an All-American halfback, averaging nearly 12 yards per carry. Ironically, his weakest sport was baseball. His base stealing and fielding were very good, but his batting average was under .200.

He was good enough, however, to obtain a tryout with the Chicago White Sox, which he attended in 1942 together with Negro League pitcher Nate Moreland. Chicago manager Jimmy Dykes was duly impressed, despite the fact that Robinson was hampered by the effects of a charley horse. "He's worth $50,000 of anybody's money," said Dykes. "He stole everything but my infielders' gloves." At the time, however, no major league team would sign a black player, no matter how good he was. No matter how much he might help their team on the field, the owners were afraid white fans would refuse to support their team if they signed a black man.

Jackie's talents extended to other sports as well. He demonstrated above-average ability in tennis, swimming, and golf. It was obvious why

Mack Robinson, Jackie's brother, wins the 200 meter dash in the far western Olympic tryouts in June 1936. His time of 21.1 seconds was one-tenth of a second better than the existing Olympic record held by Eddie Tolan.

Robinson wins the broad jump event in a May 1940 track meet at the Los Angeles Coliseum.

sportswriters began to call him "the Jim Thorpe of his race," referring to the American Indian athlete who starred in the 1912 Olympics and played major league baseball and football.

While at UCLA, Jackie met Rachel Isum, a young nursing student. They began dating and soon fell in love. With the prospect of marriage looming in the future, he decided to leave school in his senior year. He wanted to make enough money to help support his mother and, eventually, his wife and their family. He took a job with the National Youth Administration and played semi-pro football with a barnstorming team, the Los Angeles Bulldogs.

All his plans were put on hold, however, when

the Japanese bombed the U.S. Navy base at Pearl Harbor on December 7, 1941. The United States was drawn into World War II, and Robinson was drafted into the army in the spring of 1942.

Army units were then segregated according to race, and there was a great deal of prejudice throughout the armed forces as in most parts of American society. Robinson's experiences in the army included several racial confrontations. His handling of the situations revealed the character of the man who would carry the hopes of many Americans.

Upon being drafted, Robinson reported to Fort Riley, Kansas, for basic training. After completing his training, he applied for entrance into Officer's Candidate School (OCS). Despite meeting the academic requirements, Robinson was not allowed to enroll due to the Fort Riley policy forbidding entrants of his race. Rather than simply accept the decision, he decided to fight back. With the help of heavyweight boxing champion Joe Louis, who was also stationed at Fort Riley, Robinson was able to make the army change its stance, and Fort Riley's OCS opened its doors to blacks for the first time. By January 1943, he had earned his second lieutenant's bars.

Discrimination continued in different ways. Robinson could not play on the base's football team in a game against the University of Missouri because the school refused to play against a team with a black player. His attempt to join the baseball team ended when he was told he had to play with the black squad. This proved hard to do because no such team existed.

The most serious incident in Robinson's army career, however, took place in August 1944, after he had been transferred to Camp Hood in Texas.

Jackie Robinson (kneeling, second from left) is shown with his Kansas City Monarchs' teammates. The Monarchs were a perennial powerhouse in the Negro Leagues.

He was returning from town to the base by bus one day when the driver suddenly stopped and ordered him to sit in the back. Robinson refused, knowing the driver's request was a violation of a federal ruling against segregated buses on army bases.

The military police were summoned, and Robinson found himself facing a court-martial for disobedience. Although he was acquitted of all charges, Robinson found that the incident added to his growing reputation as a troublemaker. But he was never hesitant to stand up for his rights, even in the face of personal risk. As Branch Rickey would later observe, "If he had done the things people are criticizing him for as a white…he would have been praised to the skies as a fighter…but because he's black, his aggressiveness is offensive to some."

Robinson accepted an honorable discharge from the army shortly after the bus incident and returned home to continue on with his life. In 1945, he signed to play shortstop with the Kansas City

Monarchs in the Negro Leagues for $400 a month.

With the major leagues closed to black ball-players, the Negro Leagues were the only alternative for Robinson and other blacks to get paid to play ball. Traveling by bus as he barnstormed his way across the country, he viewed the future as far from bright. "If I left baseball," thought Robinson, "where could I go, what could I do to earn enough money to help my mother and to marry Rachel?"

Although he did not know it at the time, a longtime baseball man, Branch Rickey, had already set in motion the machinery that would provide him with the answer.

3

"THE MAHATMA,"
BRANCH RICKEY

Jackie Robinson with Branch Rickey (seated left), signing his Dodger contract on October 23, 1945. Two officials of the Montreal Royals look on.

According to baseball commissioner Kenesaw Mountain Landis, there was no such thing as a color line in organized baseball in 1942. "There is no rule," he declared, "formal or informal, or any understanding—unwritten, subterranean, or sub-anything—against the hiring of Negro players by the teams of organized ball." However, since 1900 no major or minor league team had placed a black on its roster.

In 1904, while serving as coach of the Ohio Wesleyan University baseball team, a 23-year-old Branch Rickey saw first-hand the problems faced by his black first baseman, Charlie Thomas. When the squad arrived in South Bend, Indiana, for a game against Notre Dame, Thomas was denied lodging at a hotel where the team had reservations. That night, Rickey watched with sadness as Thomas wept, wiping his hands as he said, "Black skin! Black skin! If I could only make them white."

"I vowed that I would always do whatever I could," Rickey later recalled, "to see that other Americans did not have to face the bitter humiliation that was heaped upon Charles Thomas."

The chance to do something about the situation arose when he came to the Brooklyn Dodgers in 1942. As president of the Dodgers, Rickey sent scouts out to scour the land for a particular type of player—someone who could help his team win and could be strong enough to face the tremendous pressures of being the first of his race in organized ball. For his plan to succeed, everything had to be perfect. Rickey later explained, "I talked to sociologists and to Negro leaders. With their counsel, I worked out what I considered to be the six essential points to be considered.

"Number one, the man we finally choose has to be right off the field. *Off* the field.

"Number two, he had to be right *on* the field. If he turned out to be a lemon, our efforts would fail for that reason alone.

"Number three, the reaction of his own race had to be right.

"Number four, the reaction of press and public had to be right.

"Number five, we had to have a place to put him.

"Number six, the reaction of his fellow players had to be right."

Scout Clyde Sukeforth was sent to check out Robinson. His recommendation: Jack Roosevelt Robinson seemed to meet all the necessary requirements, even though he was not generally considered to be the top black player of the day.

The historic first meeting between the two men took place in New York on August 28, 1945. Rickey talked in general terms about the kind of man he was looking for, and then he proceeded to subject Jackie to examples of the insults he would be likely to face as the first major league

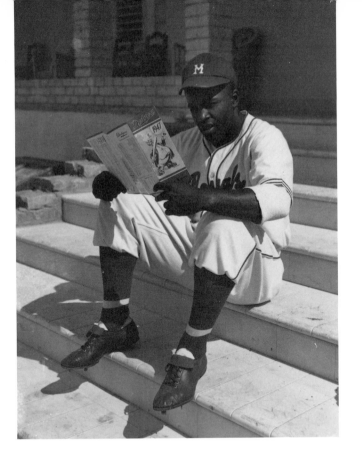

At the start of spring training in 1947 Jackie Robinson looks for his name on the Brooklyn roster. The Dodgers trained out of the country in 1947 and 1948 before buying land at Vero Beach, Florida, for a permanent spring training location.

black ballplayer in this century.

"Mr. Rickey," asked Robinson, "do you want a ballplayer who's afraid to fight back?"

"I want a player with guts enough not to fight back," replied Rickey. The player chosen needed to be strong enough to avoid confrontations on or off the field. Too many people would be looking for any excuse to keep him out of the major leagues. Even if he were provoked, a fight could ruin his chances and those of blacks for years to come.

Robinson understood Rickey's reasoning and agreed to the proposal. "If you want to take this gamble," he said, "I will promise you there will be no incident." His contract called for a bonus on signing of $3,500 and a salary of $600 a month. Robinson also agreed not to tell anyone of the deal, with the exception of Rachel and his mother.

Rickey planned to break the news to the world when the time was right.

Two months later, on Tuesday, October 23, 1945, Hector Racine, president of the Dodgers' Montreal farm club, called a press conference at the team's home ballpark. He announced that Jack Robinson had signed a contract with the Royals, setting off a furor that would echo across the country.

"Robinson is a good ballplayer," said Racine, "and comes highly recommended by the Brooklyn Dodgers. We paid him a good bonus to sign with our club."

Announcement of the historic signing was greeted with skepticism by many. New York *Daily News* columnist Jimmy Powers wrote, "We don't believe Jackie Robinson, colored college star signed by the Dodgers for one of their farm teams, will ever play in the big leagues. We question Branch Rickey's pompous statements that he [Rickey] is another Abraham Lincoln and that he has a heart as big as

Robinson and Rachel Isum were married in Los Angeles in 1946, six years after they met at UCLA.

a watermelon and he loves all mankind."

Even Cleveland Indians star pitcher Bob Feller expressed doubts about Robinson's abilities. Noting Robinson's muscular build (5 feet, 11½ inches tall, 195 pounds), and his "football shoulders," he predicted that Robinson would not be able to move his upper body fast enough to hit an inside pitch. "If he was a white man, I doubt if they would consider him big-league material," Feller said. "I hope he makes good. But I don't think he will."

Robinson and Rachel wed on February 10, 1946, in a ceremony performed by his friend the Reverend Karl Downs. With his young bride by his side, he headed to the Dodgers' camp in Florida for his first spring training. He knew he would not have an easy time of it. That winter, in fact, he had told reporters, "I know I am heading for trouble in Florida next March when I must train with Montreal. I don't look for anything physical.... I know I'll take a tongue beating, though. But I think I can take it."

The degree of hostility to be faced surprised even Rickey, however. "I didn't realize it was going to be this bad," he said. "Next year we'll have to train outside the country."

Robinson and Rachel endured the taunts of the fans and opposing players, but his first taste since the age of five of the persecution of blacks in the South must have taken its toll. He did not have a good spring, and when the Montreal Royals went north, many were doubtful that he would succeed in the pros.

Robinson's opening-day performance in Jersey City, however, put a rest to such fears. He followed up his 4-for-5 debut by hitting safely in 10 of his team's first 12 games, leading them to the top of the International League standings. He became a hero in Montreal, where fans flocked to the ballpark in record numbers. "For Jackie Robinson and the city of Montreal," wrote one reporter, "it was love at first sight."

It was very different in most American cities. Jackie was subjected to torrents of abuse with nearly every step he took. Visiting players are rarely given much respect by hometown fans or players, but he became the favorite target of opposing pitchers. "You never saw anything like it," recalled teammate Dixie Howell. "Every time he came up he went down"—meaning that pitchers tried to knock him down with a pitch. Jackie had promised Rickey *and* himself that he would not show his anger, and that he would play baseball well. And he did.

At the end of the season the Royals were in first place by 19½ games. They breezed through the International League playoffs and moved on to meet the Louisville Colonels, the American Association winner, in the Little World Series.

At Parkway Field, the Colonels' home park, few black fans were allowed in to see the games. The Louisville management claimed to be afraid that Robinson's appearance would provoke racial violence. The white fans heaped abuse on Robinson, and he responded with a subpar performance at the plate. With their most exciting player playing poorly, the Royals lost two of the three games played down South.

Back in Montreal, however, things were different.

The hometown fans at Delormier Downs inspired their heroes. Robinson responded with a game-winning single in the bottom half of the fourth game's tenth inning to give the Royals their second victory. He continued to play brilliantly over the next two games, and Montreal took the three final games of the series to win it 4 games to 2.

Following the deciding contest, the crowd spilled out onto the field and engulfed their hero. "They hugged him, kissed him, cried, cheered, and pulled and tore at his uniform while parading him around the infield on their shoulders," wrote teammate Dick Bacon. "With tears streaming down his face, Robinson finally begged off in order to shower, dress, and catch a plane to the States."

This memorable sight caused one reporter to remark, "It was probably the only day in history that a black man ran from a white mob with love, instead of lynching, on its mind."

One of the more significant comments of the day was made by Montreal manager Clay Hopper, whose family owned a Mississippi plantation. He never showed any prejudice toward his star second baseman, but Hopper had originally asked Rickey not to send Robinson to play on his team. "I'm white and I've lived in Mississippi all of my life," he said. "If you do this, you're going to force me to move my family and home out of Mississippi."

Hopper approached Robinson during the club-house celebration: "You're a great ballplayer and a fine gentleman," he told him. "It's been wonderful having you on the team."

Robinson finished the year as the International League batting champion, compiling a .349 average in 124 games. He tied for the league lead in runs scored with 113, and drove in 66 runs. His prowess in the field saw him pace the league's second basemen with a fielding percentage of .985.

Robinson appeared ready for a shot at the majors. But were the majors ready for him?

4

THE MAJORS AT LAST

To avoid the harassment that Robinson had faced the previous year, in 1947 Rickey decided to hold spring training for both Montreal and the Dodgers in Havana, Cuba. Three new black players joined Robinson on the Montreal roster—catcher Roy Campanella and pitchers Don Newcombe and Roy Partlow.

Rumors circulated in the major league club that Rickey was ready to promote Robinson to the Dodgers' roster. Unfortunately, some players on the team did not want to see a black join the club. An anti-Robinson petition was circulated, and several players signed it.

Dodgers manager Leo Durocher was furious about the petition, and Rickey made it clear where he stood on the matter. The "offended" players were offered a chance to quit the team if they could not accept a black man as their teammate. No one quit, and although it took some longer than others, nearly every one eventually came to accept and respect Robinson once he made the team.

Robinson was so popular with fans that the Dodgers hired a secretary just to answer the piles of letters addressed to him.

That spring Robinson began learning to play first base, since the Dodgers already had a standout second baseman in Eddie Stanky. Jackie had an excellent spring for Montreal, especially in exhibition games against the Dodgers. Rickey had hoped that his performance would cause the Brooklyn fans to push for him to be called up from the farm. Unfortunately, there was no such outcry.

As it became obvious that Robinson was ready for the big leagues, Rickey instructed Durocher to hint to favored reporters that the youngster could be the key to the team's pennant chances. Again, Rickey's plan did not work. On April 9th, before he could plant the seed in the minds of the reporters, Durocher was suspended from baseball by Albert "Happy" Chandler, who succeeded Landis as baseball commissioner, for his association with known gamblers.

During the ruckus that followed the commissioner's announcement, Rickey made his move. On April 10th, a press release was distributed in the press box: "Brooklyn announces the purchase of the contract of Jack Roosevelt Robinson from Montreal.... He will report immediately."

On April 15, 1947, the Dodgers took the field against the visiting Boston Braves for their season opener. After Clyde Sukeforth managed for one game, Burt Shotton was named permanent manager. Jackie Robinson started at first base and wore uniform number 42. Included among the crowd of 26,623 at Ebbets Field that day were Jackie's wife, Rachel, and the couple's infant son, Jackie, Jr.

Understandably, Robinson was jittery. "I was nervous on my first day in my first game at Ebbets Field," he would later recall, "but nothing has bothered me since."

Robinson looks on approvingly at the left-handed batting stance of Jackie Robinson, Jr.

Despite immediate acceptance by the Brooklyn fans, he proceeded to go hitless in three at bats in his debut. He handled 11 chances in the field without an error and scored one run, as the Dodgers rallied for three runs in the bottom half of the seventh inning to post a 5–3 victory. "I know the crowd was pulling for me," he told *New York Post* columnist Jimmy Cannon. "I could hear them at first base.... I hope I can keep them with me by playing some baseball for them."

In his second game, Robinson managed a bunt single for his first big-league hit. When the team traveled across the river to the Polo Grounds to play New York City's other National League team, the Giants, he smacked his first major league home run to lead the Dodgers to a 10-to-4 victory over their biggest rivals.

Large numbers of blacks were coming to the games, and Robinson did not disappoint them. He went 3 for 4 the next day in front of a record Saturday afternoon crowd of more than 52,000 people. When the Dodgers finally returned from their road trip, their first opponents were the

Philadelphia Phillies. This series saw the most bitter personal attack that Robinson received from any team.

Alabama-born Ben Chapman, the manager of the Phillies, made no secret of his dislike for blacks. He encouraged his players to deluge the Dodgers first baseman with curses and insults of all types from the opening minute of the first game of the series. Even veteran baseball observers had never heard the like of the curses that streamed from the Philadelphia dugout. Dodgers secretary Harold Parrott wrote, "At no time in my life have I heard racial venom and dugout abuse to match the abuse that Ben sprayed on Robinson that night."

Despite the bullying, Robinson kept himself under control and ignored the insults. Although at first he said the bench-jockeying did not upset him, he later conceded, "I have to admit that this day of all the unpleasant days of my life brought me nearer to cracking up than I have ever been."

Robinson scores on Carl Furillo's double in game 3 of the 1947 World Series against the Yankees. The Dodgers won 9-8.

Knowing that he could not protect himself, Jackie's teammates came to his defense and returned Philadelphia's abuse. Chapman's attempt at unnerving the rookie backfired: The Dodgers rallied together and became closer as a team than they had been before.

Robinson's acceptance was perhaps best epitomized by his relationship with Dodgers shortstop Pee Wee Reese. Since Reese was born in Kentucky, his background and position on the team seemed to provide the ideal situation in which friction would develop. In fact, when Reese originally found out that the Dodgers had signed Robinson, he joked, "Just my luck, the first Negro to be signed to a contract in modern organized baseball not only had to be signed by the Brooklyn organization, but he also had to be a shortstop."

Observing how well Robinson handled the insults and abuse, Reese went out of his way to silence Robinson's critics. When Boston fans demanded to know how a Southern gentleman such as Reese could play with a black teammate, Pee Wee responded by walking over to Robinson and putting his arm around him in a gesture of friendship and support.

Unfortunately, the problems facing the rookie did not end after that first Philadelphia game. Vicious verbal attacks from opposing players and fans continued, and the threat of violence followed him around the league. The hate mail he received often included death threats.

In early May, word leaked out of a proposed strike by St. Louis Cardinals players. They were thinking of refusing to play Brooklyn until the Dodgers dropped Robinson. National League president Ford Frick nipped the boycott in the bud. His views on the matter were clear: "I do not care

Robinson led National League first basemen in turning double plays in 1947. Shown with Robinson are the other Dodger infielders: (left to right) Spider Jorgenson, Pee Wee Reese and Eddie Stanky.

if half the league strikes," he said. "Those who do it will encounter quick retribution. They will be suspended, and I don't care if it wrecks the National League for five years.... The National League will go down the line with Robinson whatever the consequence."

With the support of the league office and his teammates, Robinson began to relax and consistently play up to his potential. He played with a flair not often seen before, leading his team to victory after victory with his daring play. White and black fans packed into stadiums in record numbers to see him in action, as he erased all doubts about a black man's ability to play in the major leagues. His exploits even drew a begrudging compliment from Ben Chapman. "He's a major leaguer in every respect," admitted the Phillies' manager.

Ironically, the enthusiastic support of the black fans worried both Robinson and Rickey to a degree. Rickey decided to meet with leaders of the black

community. He would later write:

> I explained that in order to give this boy his
> chance, there must be no demonstration in his
> behalf, no excursions from one city to another,
> no presentations or testimonials. He was to be
> left alone to do this thing without any more
> hazards than were already present. For two
> years, the men I talked to respected the reason-
> ing behind my requests. My admiration for these
> men is limitless. In the best possible way, they
> saw to it that Jackie Robinson had his chance to
> make it on his own.

To American blacks, Robinson became a symbol
of both hope and pride; they filled major league
ballparks as never before.

Robinson's intensity brought a new dimen-
sion to baseball. Not since the days of Ty Cobb
had the game seen someone whose inner fires
burned so brightly. Pittsburgh slugger Ralph
Kiner summed up the feelings of many who saw

him on the field. "Robinson was the only player I ever saw, " he said, "who could completely turn a game around by himself."

Robinson's competitiveness did not go unnoticed by the umpires, either. "He was the most difficult ballplayer I had to deal with as an umpire," wrote Jocko Conlan. "Jackie was one of those players who could never accept a decision."

Robinson's popularity was such that on September 23rd, with the permission of the Dodgers, his admirers staged a Jackie Robinson Day for him at Ebbets Field. He was showered with an estimated $10,000 worth of gifts from fans across the country.

Sparked by his play, the Dodgers had emerged as the team to beat in the National League. They went on to clinch the pennant and finished the season five games ahead of the runner-up St. Louis Cardinals. His value to the team was undeniable. "If it wasn't for him," said St. Louis second baseman Red Schoendienst, "the Dodgers would be in the second division."

Robinson batted .297 for the year, finished second in runs scored with 125, and led the league in stolen bases with 29—more than twice the total of teammate Pete Reiser, who finished second.

Nineteen forty-seven was the first time the Rookie of the Year Award was given. The prize is voted on by the Baseball Writers Association of America, and Robinson easily beat out the best new players in both leagues. (Two years later, each league would have an award.) He also totaled 106 points in the voting for the National League's Most Valuable Player award, finishing in fifth place.

The Dodgers faced the New York Yankees in the World Series that fall, and they lost to the

"Bronx Bombers" in seven exciting games. But for Robinson the series was anticlimactic. Baseball's "great experiment" to test if a black man could play major league baseball had, indeed, been a success.

5

SPEAKING OUT

Nineteen forty-eight was a year of change for Robinson and the Dodgers. Veteran Eddie Stanky was traded to the Boston Braves in March. Robinson became the team's regular second baseman, although he still appeared in 30 games at first base, and 6 at third. Leo Durocher returned from his one-year suspension to replace Burt Shotton as manager.

Roy Campanella joined the Dodgers as the team's second black player. Cleveland's Larry Doby had broken the color line in the American League the year before, and other blacks were set to follow the path blazed by Robinson.

In mid-July, with the team playing .500 ball, Durocher shocked the baseball world by signing to manage the New York Giants, Brooklyn's hated crosstown rival. When Shotton returned to take over as field leader, the club improved in the

Robinson (left) with Don Newcombe and Roy Campanella. The three stars helped the Dodgers win five pennants in the decade before the Dodgers moved to Los Angeles at the end of 1957.

standings but still finished a disappointing third behind the Boston Braves and St. Louis.

Like the Dodgers, Robinson started out slowly. He came on strong at the end of the season and finished with a .296 batting average, a stolen base total of 22, 58 extra base hits, and 108 runs scored. In the field, he had no trouble mastering his new position, and he led the league's second basemen in fielding.

That winter, Branch Rickey came to an important decision. For two years he had watched Robinson take all the abuse opposing teams had to offer. For two years Robinson had been a perfect gentleman, keeping his temper in check in an exemplary manner. Rickey knew that some saw Robinson's refusal to fight back as a sign of weakness and looked to take advantage of it. As Jules Tygiel recounted in *Baseball's Great Experi-*

After stealing second base, Robinson scored on a wild throw by Giants' catcher Wes Westrum. Robinson led the league in stolen bases in two of his first three years.

ment, Rickey realized that these people "could be made to respect only the fighting back, the things that are the signs of courage to men who know courage only in its physical sense."

Rickey felt his second baseman had suffered silently for long enough. "Jackie, you're on your own now, you can be yourself now."

A changed man appeared at the 1949 spring training. Jackie announced to the reporters covering the Dodgers that opposing teams "better be rough on me this year, because I'm sure going to be rough on them."

He proceeded to wreak havoc throughout the National League. He batted a career-high .342 to win the batting title and also finished on top in stolen bases with 37. His 124 runs batted in and 203 hits were second best in the league. He finished in the top five in runs scored (122), doubles (38), triples (12), total bases (313), and slugging percentage (.528).

Black pitcher Don Newcombe won 17 games to take Rookie of the Year honors, and the Dodgers edged the St. Louis Cardinals by one game for the National League pennant, defeating Philadelphia 9 to 7 in ten innings on the last day of the season. For his play on the field, Robinson was named the league's Most Valuable Player. Rickey rewarded his star with a significant raise. Jackie's 1950 contract would pay him $35,000.

In addition, Robinson joined Campanella, Newcombe, and Doby as the first blacks to play in an All-Star Game. He had a double in four at bats in the contest, scoring three runs as the National League lost to the American by 11 to 7.

The Dodgers' season ended on a low note, however, as the team lost the World Series to the New York Yankees, 4 games to 1. Brooklyn fans would once again lament, "Wait 'til next year!"

Off the field, Robinson was no longer timid about stating his social and political beliefs. In July, he testified before Congress about the role of blacks in the military:

> I've got too much invested for my wife and child and myself in the future of this country [not to fight], and I and other Americans of many races and faiths have too much invested in our country's welfare, for any of us to throw it away.... But that doesn't mean we're going to stop fighting race discrimination in this country until we've got it licked. It means that we're going to fight it all the harder because our stake in the future is so big.

Nineteen fifty began on a positive note for the Robinsons. In January, Rachel gave birth to their second child, daughter Sharon. Early 1950 also marked Jackie's debut as a movie actor. Hollywood was filming *The Jackie Robinson Story*, and he had been asked to play himself. Although the movie did not get good reviews, he enjoyed his experience in California.

Life on the baseball field continued to be difficult. A Cincinnati fan threatened to shoot him the next time he appeared on the field. His teammates helped him through this tense situation as only teammates can. They joked that they would all wear his number 42 on their uniforms to confuse the gunman.

Jackie again led National League second basemen in fielding, while batting .328, scoring 99 runs, and driving in 81. The Dodgers' season could not be considered quite as successful. They lost the pennant to Philadelphia's "Whiz Kids" despite a strong stretch run that saw them close to within one game of the top on the season's last day.

Needing a victory over the Phils to gain a tie and force a playoff, the Dodgers lost a 4–1 heartbreaker in 10 innings.

In addition to the tough loss, Robinson had another "loss" to think about over the winter: On October 26th, Branch Rickey resigned as president of the Dodgers. Walter O'Malley was introduced as the new president of the team. Looking to get rid of all reminders of his predecessor, O'Malley began by firing manager Burt Shotton and replacing him with Chuck Dressen. Robinson announced his continued loyalty to the man who had brought him to the majors, thereby incurring O'Malley's wrath.

Despite the turmoil in the front office, the 1951 season began on a high note for Brooklyn. The team jumped to the top of the league standings. By early August, their lead was an impressive 13½ games over the Giants.

What happened from that point on, however, is something Dodgers fans would prefer to forget. The

Giants, managed by Leo Durocher, made an incredible stretch run, winning 37 of their last 44 games to move into first. For the second year in a row the Dodgers' post-season hopes depended on the outcome of the regular season's last game. They needed a victory to assure themselves of a tie with the Giants. On the last day of the season, they again faced the Phillies.

This game was to be one of Robinson's greatest.

Philadelphia jumped out to an early lead and was ahead 6 to 1 after three innings. The Dodgers rallied to tie, with Jackie's two-run triple in the fifth a key blow, and the score stood at 8–8 going into extra innings.

With the bases loaded and two outs in the twelfth, Robinson saved the game for Brooklyn with a diving catch of a line drive off the bat of Eddie Waitkus. He lay still on the ground, the wind knocked out of him. When he finally stood up, the ball appeared, firmly wedged in his mitt.

Number 42 Robinson looks on from his second-base position as Bobby Thomson scores after hitting his dramatic home run to win the 1951 pennant for the Giants.

The pressure built with each succeeding inning. Jackie came to bat in the fourteenth with two outs and nobody on base. Facing 21-game winner (and future Hall of Famer) Robin Roberts, he proceeded to drive a 1-and-1 pitch into the left field stands for the game winner.

The Dodgers and Giants would now meet in a three-game playoff to determine the National League pennant.

The teams split the first two games. In the deciding game Robinson drove in the first run of the contest in the opening inning. Brooklyn carried a 4-to-1 lead into the ninth.

But in the bottom half of the inning, in what is arguably the most dramatic moment in the history of baseball, Bobby Thomson hit a three-run-homer—the "Shot Heard 'Round the World"—to cap a four-run rally and give the Giants the game—and the pennant.

Once more it was a devastating climax to the season. And once more Jackie compiled solid statistics, finishing third in the league in batting average (.338), doubles (33), and stolen bases (25). He also scored 106 runs and drove home 88, while leading National League second basemen in fielding average for the third time in four years.

Hopes for a World Championship would have to wait for another day.

6

A TITLE FOR BROOKLYN

As he became more and more outspoken, Robinson's popularity with the media began to decline. The press compared him unfavorably with black teammate Roy Campanella, who was praised for his quiet demeanor. Jackie replied with the intense pride that marked his personality. "If [my aggressiveness] makes some people uncomfortable," he said, "if it makes me the kind of guy they can't like, that's tough."

His fiery performance on the field continued to spark the Dodgers. In 1952 they once again won the National League pennant. Robinson ended the season with a .308 average, 19 home runs, 75 runs batted in, and 24 stolen bases. He also garnered a career-high 106 bases on balls, which helped him to score 100 runs for the fifth time in his six years in the majors. For the fourth straight year, he was named second baseman on *The Sporting*

Robinson steals home in the eighth inning of game 1 of the 1955 World Series. Yogi Berra attempts the tag for the Yankees as Dodgers pinchhitter Frank Kellert watches.

News All-Star Major League Team.

The Dodgers' opponent in the 1952 World Series was again the mighty New York Yankees. Robinson homered in Brooklyn's victory in game 1, but batted only .174 overall. The Yankees won the series 4 games to 3 for their fifteenth world championship. The Dodgers were still looking for their first world title.

Robinson made his first concession to age the next year. Although he continued to amass impressive numbers at the plate, he had begun to lose a step in the field. In 1953 he played 76 games in the outfield and 44 at third base, positions not so wearing on the 34-year-old veteran. Rookie Jim "Junior" Gilliam, another Negro League graduate, took his place at second base.

The Dodgers were the class of the league, winning a franchise record 105 games and finishing 13 games ahead of the transplanted Braves in their first year in Milwaukee. A vital cog in the Dodgers' potent attack, Jackie drove in 95 runs, scored 109, hit 12 homers, and batted .329.

But, as in previous years, the Dodgers' quest for a World Championship was cut short by the Yankees. The Bronx Bombers defeated them in six games in the fall classic, despite Robinson's .320 batting mark.

Off the field, he continued to speak his mind about racial prejudice. During a November appearance on the television program "Youth Wants to Know," Robinson was asked if he thought the Yankees were prejudiced against blacks. His reply was straight to the point. "I think the Yankee management is prejudiced," he answered. "There isn't a single Negro on the team now and very few in the entire Yankee farm system."

Although he was criticized by many, baseball

commissioner Ford Frick let him know that the commissioner's office would support his right to speak out on racial issues. He was becoming more and more of a spokesman on behalf of American blacks.

That winter, after having won two consecutive pennants, Dodgers manager Chuck Dressen asked for a three-year contract. When owner Walter O'Malley refused, Dressen quit. Walter Alston, a minor league manager in the Dodgers' system for 10 years, was chosen to guide the club for the 1954 season.

Friction soon developed between star and manager. Alston's style of playing baseball according to the percentages did not mesh well with Robinson's preference for risk taking.

In addition, he missed Dressen, calling him the best manager he ever played for. His spirits may have been low, but he again posted All-Star statis-

Robinson was the target of racist threats and hate mail for much of his major-league career.

tics. Splitting time between the outfield and third base, he batted .311 in 124 games, while stroking 15 home runs. His stolen base total, however, dropped to a career low of 7.

The New York Giants, sparked by Willie Mays, raced to the 1954 pennant. The Dodgers finished in second place, five games behind. As Robinson neared the end of his career, it began to appear that he might never again have the chance to play for the title.

Discrimination away from the game also weighed heavily on his mind. Since their second son, David, had been born in 1952, the Robinsons had been looking for a larger home for their family. They had moved from Brooklyn to Queens, and now looked to relocate in the suburbs. But it was not until a newspaper story mentioned that racial prejudice often denied them a chance to look at homes available to white buyers that they were able to buy a house in a well-to-do section of Stamford, Connecticut.

Brooklyn began the 1955 season with high

The fiery Robinson kept his temper with umpires for nearly two seasons. It was not until September 1948, when umpire Butch Henline ejected him, that Robinson was thrown out of a game. Robinson hailed the act as a sign of acceptance.

hopes. Powered by the hitting of Duke Snider, Roy Campanella, Gil Hodges, and Carl Furillo, the team pulled away form the rest of the league, winning 22 of their first 24 games. Headed by 20-game winner Don Newcombe, the pitching staff combined to record the league's best earned run average. It soon became apparent that the only question remaining was by how many games the club would win the pennant.

Robinson was spending most of his time at third base now, sharing the duties with Don Hoak. He appeared in a career-low 105 games and batted only .256. Despite those numbers, the Dodgers rolled over the rest of the league, clinching the pennant on September 8th and finishing 13½ games ahead of the Braves. The Yankees would again be their Series opponents, for the fifth time in nine seasons.

The Dodgers fought valiantly, but came up short in the opener at Yankee Stadium, losing 6–5. When the Bronx Bombers also proceeded to take the second game, many Brooklyn fans began to give up on their team for another year.

But the Dodgers refused to be counted out. They came back to sweep the three games played in Ebbets Field and headed back to the Bronx, where the Yankees tied the series by winning game 6. The two teams would face off in one final game to decide the crown, as they had in both the 1947 and the 1952 World Series.

The difference was that this time the Dodgers came out on top. Dodgers left-hander Johnny Podres shut out the Yankees 2 to 0 in the final game to give the Brooklyn franchise its first—and only—World Championship. "It was one of the greatest thrills of my life," said Robinson, "to be finally on a World Series winner."

"Next year" had finally arrived.

The following season would prove to be Robinson's last in the majors. Jackie, age 37, batted just .275 in a part-time role. The Dodgers clinched the pennant on the last day of the season and moved on to the World Series again. Their opponents, as usual, were the New York Yankees.

The New Yorkers exacted revenge for their 1955 Series loss by defeating the Dodgers, 4 games to 3. The highlight of the match-up was Yankee Don Larsen's perfect game in game 5. No Dodger reached base as the big right-hander performed a feat not seen before—or since—in the fall classic. The closest the Dodgers came to getting a baserunner was when Robinson, batting in the clean-up position, led off the second inning. He lined a shot off Yankees third baseman Andy Carey that caromed over to shortstop Gil McDougald. McDougald threw to first, nipping him by a half step.

Robinson's one last moment of glory came in game 6. With the game scoreless in the bottom half of the tenth inning, he hit a fly ball that was misjudged by left fielder Enos Slaughter. The ball fell in for a single, driving in the only run of the game and tying the series. It would be Robinson's last major league hit, as he went hitless in game 7.

Throughout the course of the season, Robinson had pondered his future, seriously giving thought to retirement. He had been offered a job as vice-president of community relations with Chock Full O'Nuts, a large New York restaurant chain.

But on December 13, before he had a chance to accept the offer, the Dodgers made a startling announcement: Robinson had been traded to the New York Giants in exchange for journeyman pitcher Dick Littlefield and $30,000. "We hate to lose Jackie," announced Walter O'Malley in defense of the deal, "but it is necessary for the good of the team."

The thought of Robinson in a New York Giants uniform was a difficult one for Brooklyn fans to imagine. The Giants, who had fallen to sixth place in 1956, had visions of Robinson teaming up with their young superstar, Willie Mays, to bring new excitement to the Polo Grounds. In an attempt to entice Robinson, they offered him a $40,000 contract for 1957, then $20,000 for each of the next two years as a part-time scout. For an aging ballplayer, the offer was hard to turn down.

But turn it down was exactly what he did.

The Giants increased their offer, but Robinson would not budge. "It would be unfair to the Giants and their fans to take their money," he responded. "The Giants are a team that needs youth and rebuilding. The team doesn't need me."

He ended his career with numbers worthy of an All-Star performer. In 10 big-league seasons, Robinson compiled a batting average of .311, surpassing the .300 mark six consecutive years. He recorded over 1,500 hits and scored nearly 1,000 runs. With 137 home runs and 734 runs batted in, his power totals were nothing to be ashamed of. He stole 197 bases in his career, including an incredible 19 steals of home.

His record in six All-Star Games attested to his abilities. He batted .333, with 6 hits in 18 at bats, 7 runs scored, 2 doubles, 1 home run, and 4 runs batted in.

All this from a man who did not play his first big league game until the age of 28.

Robinson's 1954 Topps bubblegum card

7

LIFE AFTER BASEBALL

Robinson eagerly looked forward to his new career with Chock Full O'Nuts. He had insisted that his position be one that required his involvement in administration. He did not want to be a figurehead, employed by the company solely for the publicity value of his name.

He worked for the betterment of the employees and the community, standing behind his belief that "there were two keys to the advancement of blacks in America—the ballot and the buck."

He became an important figure in the civil rights movement, acting as a spokesman and fundraiser for the National Association for the Advancement of Colored People (NAACP). He called upon blacks to become more active in the business community, and did so himself. In addition to his work with Chock Full O' Nuts, he participated in black-owned community ventures such as the Freedom Bank in Harlem and the Jackie Robinson Construction Corporation.

He also took a more active role in politics, campaigning for Republican Party nominee Richard Nixon in the 1960 presidential race. This

Jackie Robinson lends his moral support to a 1963 picket march in support of equal rights in hiring.

In 1982, the United States postal service issued a Jackie Robinson stamp. He is one of four major-leaguers to be so honored.

eventually led to a close relationship with New York governor Nelson Rockefeller, who appointed Robinson his Special Assistant for Community Affairs.

In 1962, Robinson became eligible for election into baseball's Hall of Fame in Cooperstown, New York. He was elected in his first year of eligibility, with his name appearing on 124 of the 160 ballots cast by the Baseball Writers Association of America. Deep down inside, he was surprised at being chosen. "Since I was a controversial personality in the eyes of the press," he said, "I steeled myself for rejection."

He was officially inducted that summer along with Cleveland great Bob Feller.

Despite his financial, athletic, and business successes and the honors that had been bestowed upon him, Robinson was not as happy a person as one might have expected. He and his eldest son had grown further and further apart. "I loved him deeply and he knew it," said Robinson. "But the peculiar chemistry that is responsible for free communication between two individuals was absent."

In 1964, the youngster joined the army and went off to fight in Vietnam.

A string of tragedies followed. Branch Rickey, Robinson's old mentor, died in 1965 at the age of 83, and Robinson's mother passed away three years later.

In the meantime, Jackie, Jr., had returned home from the service in 1967, having been wounded in action. His experiences in the war left him with even deeper psychological wounds. He became addicted to drugs, although he refused to admit it at the time. The extent of his problem became public knowledge the next year, when he was arrested for possession of drugs and for carrying a concealed weapon.

The father knew his son desperately needed his support. "I realized I had been so busy trying to help other youngsters," he said, "that I had neglected my own." Jackie, Jr., entered a rehabilitation program, where he began to face up to his problems.

Upon completion of the program, Jackie, Jr., decided to dedicate himself to helping other addicts. He got a job as a counselor and had just begun to get his life back in order when tragedy struck again: On June 17, 1971, he was killed in an automobile accident.

The death of his son symbolized the beginning of the end for Jackie Robinson. "You just don't lose a boy after finding him again and not really feel it," he reflected.

His body began to wear down seemingly all at once. The ravages of diabetes and heart disease limited his mobility and robbed him of most of his eyesight. In June 1972, when he was honored at Dodger Stadium during a ceremony marking the 25th anniversary of his major league debut, he was but a shell of his former self.

On October 24, 1972, at the age of 53, Jackie Robinson died of a heart attack at his home in Stamford, Connecticut.

The legacy he left behind will remain as long as young boys and girls continue to play ball and dream of the major leagues. Jack Roosevelt Robinson fought for the right of each and every one of them to have the chance to live out their dreams.

"A life is not important," he often said, "except in the impact it has on others."

If that is true, then few men have led more important lives than Jackie Robinson.

CHRONOLOGY

Jan. 31, 1919	Jack Roosevelt Robinson is born in Cairo, Georgia.
May, 1923	Robinson family moves to Pasadena, California.
Sept., 1937	Enrolls at Pasadena Junior College.
Sept., 1939	Enrolls at UCLA.
1942	Receives tryout with Chicago White Sox.
1942–1944	Serves in the U.S. Army.
1945	Plays Negro League ball with the Kansas City Monarchs.
Aug. 28, 1945	Meets with Branch Rickey and signs contract to play with the Montreal Royals of the International League.
Feb. 10, 1946	Marries Rachel Isum.
April 18, 1946	Plays first game for the Montreal Royals.
Nov. 18, 1946	Jackie Robinson, Jr., is born.
April 15, 1947	Makes his big-league debut against the Boston Braves at Ebbets Field. Grounds out against Johnny Sain in his first at bat.
Oct., 1947	Voted National League Rookie of the Year.
1949	Named National League Most Valuable Player. Wins batting title with .342 average.
Jan. 13, 1950	Sharon Robinson is born.
1950	Stars in film biography, *The Jackie Robinson Story*.
May 14, 1952	David Robinson is born.
1955	Robinson family moves to Stamford, Connecticut. Dodgers win the World Series.
Dec. 13, 1956	Dodgers trade Robinson to New York Giants in exchange for pitcher Dick Littlefield and $30,000.
Jan., 1957	Announces his retirement from baseball.
1957	Joins Chock Full O'Nuts as vice-president of community relations.
1960	Campaigns for Richard Nixon for President.
Jan. 23, 1962	Elected to baseball's Hall of Fame.
1968	Robinson's mother dies.
June 17, 1971	Robinson's son Jackie, Jr., is killed in an automobile accident.
Oct. 24, 1972	Robinson dies of a heart attack in Stamford, Connecticut.

JACK ROOSEVELT ROBINSON

BROOKLYN N.L. 1947 TO 1956

LEADING N.L. BATTER IN 1949. HOLDS
FIELDING MARK FOR SECOND BASEMAN
PLAYING IN 150 OR MORE GAMES WITH .992.
LED N.L. IN STOLEN BASES IN 1947 AND
1949. MOST VALUABLE PLAYER IN 1949.
LIFETIME BATTING AVERAGE .311. JOINT
RECORD HOLDER FOR MOST DOUBLE PLAYS
BY SECOND BASEMAN, 137 IN 1951.
LED SECOND BASEMEN IN DOUBLE
PLAYS 1949-50-51-52.

MAJOR LEAGUE STATISTICS

BROOKLYN DODGERS

Year	Team	G	AB	R	H	2B	3B	HR	RBI	BA	SB
1947	BKN N	151	590	125	175	31	5	12	48	.297	29
1948		147	574	108	170	38	8	12	85	.296	22
1949		156	593	122	203	38	12	16	124	.342	37
1950		144	518	99	170	39	4	14	81	.328	12
1951		153	548	106	185	33	7	19	88	.338	25
1952		149	510	104	157	17	3	19	75	.308	24
1953		136	484	109	159	34	7	12	95	.329	17
1954		124	386	62	120	22	4	15	59	.311	7
1955		105	317	51	81	6	2	8	36	.256	12
1956		117	357	61	98	15	2	10	43	.275	12
Totals		1382	4877	947	1518	273	54	137	734	.311	197
World Series 6 years		38	137	22	32	7	1	2	12	.234	6
All-Star Games 6 years		6	18	7	6	2	0	1	4	.333	0

FURTHER READING

Adler, David A. *Jackie Robinson: He Was the First.* New York: Holiday House, 1989.

Frommer, Harvey. *Rickey and Robinson: The Men Who Broke Baseball's Color Barrier.* New York: Macmillan, 1982.

Holmes, Tommy. *The Dodgers.* New York: Rutledge Books, 1975.

Kahn, Roger. *The Boys of Summer.* New York: New American Library, 1973.

Mann, Arthur. *The Jackie Robinson Story.* New York: Grosset & Dunlap, 1951.

Okrent, Daniel, and Harris Lewine, eds. *The Ultimate Baseball Book.* Boston: Houghton Mifflin, 1979.

Robinson, Jackie, and Alfred Duckett. *I Never Had It Made.* New York: Fawcett Crest, 1974.

Robinson, Jackie, and Wendell Smith. *Jackie Robinson: My Own Story.* New York: Greenberg, 1948.

Roeder, Bill. *Jackie Robinson.* New York: A. S. Barnes, 1950.

Rowan, Carl T., with Jackie Robinson....*Wait Till Next Year.* New York: Random House, 1960.

Scott, Richard. *Jackie Robinson.* New York: Chelsea House, 1987.

Shapiro, Milton J. *Jackie Robinson of the Brooklyn Dodgers.* New York: Julian Messner, 1957.

Tiemann, Robert L. *Dodger Classics.* St. Louis: Baseball Histories, 1983.

Tygiel, Jules. *Baseball's Great Experiment: Jackie Robinson and His Legacy.* New York: Vintage, 1984.

INDEX

JOHN F. GRABOWSKI was educated at the City College of New York, where he was a member of the baseball team, and at Teachers College, Columbia University, where he received his master's in educational psychology. He currently teaches high school math and computer studies on Staten Island. He is a free-lance writer who has had several hundred pieces published in newspapers, magazines, and the programs of professional teams. The author of *Super Sports Word Find Puzzles*, *Dodgers Trivia*, *Cleveland Browns Trivia*, *San Francisco 49ers Trivia*, and *Detroit Tigers Trivia*, he published the monthly *Baseball Trivia Newsletter*. A nationally syndicated columnist, his weekly "Stat Sheet" is supplied to more than 600 newspapers by Newspaper Enterprise Association.

JIM MURRAY, veteran sports columnist of the *Los Angeles Times*, is one of America's most acclaimed writers. He has been named "America's Best Sportswriter" by the National Association of Sportscasters and Sportswriters 14 times, was awarded the Red Smith Award, and was twice winner of the National Headliner Award. In addition, he was awarded the J. G. Taylor Spink Award in 1987 for "meritorious contributions to baseball writing." With this award came his 1988 induction into the National Baseball Hall of Fame in Cooperstown, New York. In 1990, Jim Murray was awarded the Pulitzer Prize for Commentary.

EARL WEAVER is the winningest manager in Baltimore Orioles history by a wide margin. He compiled 1,480 victories in his 17 years at the helm. After managing eight different minor league teams, he was given the chance to lead the Orioles in 1968. Under his leadership the Orioles finished lower than second place in the American League East only four times in 17 years. One of only 12 managers in big league history to have managed in four or more World Series, Earl was named Manager of the Year in 1979. The popular Weaver had his number 5 retired in 1982, joining Brooks Robinson, Frank Robinson, and Jim Palmer, whose numbers were retired previously. Earl Weaver continues his association with the professional baseball scene by writing, broadcasting, and coaching.